# POETRY
# ESCAPE

## POEMS FROM THE SOUTH

Edited By Jess Giaffreda

First published in Great Britain in 2019 by:

Young Writers
Remus House
Coltsfoot Drive
Peterborough
PE2 9BF
Telephone: 01733 890066
Website: www.youngwriters.co.uk

# FOREWORD

Since 1991 our aim here at Young Writers has been to encourage creativity in children and young adults and to inspire a love of the written word. Each competition is tailored to the relevant age group, hopefully giving each student the inspiration and incentive to create their own piece of creative writing, whether it's a poem or a short story. We truly believe that seeing their work in print gives students a sense of achievement and pride.

For our latest competition Poetry Escape, we challenged secondary school students to free their creativity and escape the maze of their minds using poetic techniques as their tools of navigation. They had several pathways to choose from, with each one offering either a specific theme or a writing constraint. Alternatively they could forge their own route, because there's no such thing as a dead end where imagination is concerned.

The result is an inspiring anthology full of ideas, hopes, fears and imagination, proving that creativity really does offer escape, in whatever form you need it.

We encourage young writers to express themselves and address topics that matter to them, which sometimes means exploring sensitive or difficult topics. If you have been affected by any issues raised in this book, details on where to find help can be found at: **www.youngwriters.co.uk/support.**

# CONTENTS

## Buckler's Mead Academy, Yeovil

| | |
|---|---|
| Skye Manley (12) | 66 |
| Kai Jackson (12) | 67 |
| Erin Tanswell (12) | 68 |
| Jamie-Leigh Rose (12) | 69 |
| Georgia Feast (12) | 70 |
| Lily Rose Taylor (12) | 71 |
| Noah Brian Vince (13) | 72 |
| Josh Dey (12) | 73 |
| Brooke Williams (12) | 74 |
| Connie Dopson (12) | 75 |
| Cody Isaacs (13) | 76 |
| Charlotte Sarah Chant (12) | 77 |
| Ethan John Atkins (12) | 78 |
| Erin Lillia Parsons (12) | 79 |

## Chiltern Academy, 1-9

| | |
|---|---|
| Layla Mburu (11) | 80 |
| Saadia Naser (11) | 82 |
| Sreesha Sri Ramoju (12) | 84 |
| Labib Khan (11) | 86 |
| Kumayl Abbas Naqvi (11) | 87 |
| Christiana Arsine (11) | 88 |
| Meriem Hammoun (12) | 90 |
| Haleema Naeem (11) | 91 |
| Aadam Mohammed Imran (11) | 92 |
| Ashantia Marie Fearon (11) | 93 |
| Amilia Gillas (11) | 94 |
| Isabella Lismanis (11) | 95 |
| Krystal Kankonde (11) | 96 |
| Muhammad Riyadh Hamid (11) | 97 |
| Maryam Rezzag-Lebza (11) | 98 |
| Zain Shan (11) | 99 |
| Tanisha Chowdhury (12) | 100 |
| Hasan Mahmud Chowdhury (11) | 101 |
| Mariyah Naser (11) | 102 |
| Cleopatra Attah (12) | 103 |
| Emilia Weronika Nizankowska (11) | 104 |
| Tasmiyah Chowdhury (11) | 105 |
| Makayda Williams (11) | 106 |
| Lauren Gibson (11) | 107 |

| | |
|---|---|
| Matthew Orisakwe (11) | 108 |
| Rayann Chalouache (11) | 109 |

## Harlington Upper School, Harlington

| | |
|---|---|
| Mia Kenny (14) | 110 |
| Abbie Louise Giles (15) | 112 |
| Isabelle Brown (16) | 114 |
| Aoife Murphy (14) | 116 |
| Michelle Danga (14) | 117 |
| Daisy Webb (14) | 118 |

## Hawley Hurst School, Blackwater

| | |
|---|---|
| Lisa Duke (12) | 119 |
| Amelie King (13) | 120 |
| Aryan Patel (12) | 122 |
| Siya Sardar (12) | 124 |
| Vidhita Walia (12) | 125 |
| Joshua Brooks (12) | 126 |
| Layla Aykac (13) | 128 |
| Violet Marie Stokes (12) | 129 |
| Oscar Sasso (13) | 130 |
| Olivia Marven (13) | 131 |
| Annabelle Fordham (13) | 132 |
| Ruby Emma Welch (13) | 133 |
| Lucy Chambers (13) | 134 |
| Sofia Duggan (12) | 135 |
| Sophia Wallis (12) | 136 |
| George Benedict Herbert (13) | 137 |
| George Allington (11) | 138 |
| Oliver Hounsham (13) | 139 |
| Will Bennett (13) | 140 |
| Megan Glover (12) | 141 |
| Harriet Clowes (13) | 142 |
| Louis Davies (11) | 143 |
| Cameron Frain (12) | 144 |
| Hennie Lamers (13) | 145 |
| Alyssa Day (11) | 146 |
| Miah Greenslade-Jones (12) | 147 |
| Zaynah Faruque (13) | 148 |
| Lottie Hill (12) | 149 |
| Savannah Everidge (11) | 150 |

Surya Ray-Chaudhuri (11)    151
William Carter (12)    152

## Mayfield School, Portsmouth

Tareef Ahmed (14)    153
Emma Boddy (13)    155

## Orchardside School, Enfield

Stefania Enciu (13)    157

## Priory School Specialist Sports College, Southsea

Maliha Khatun (11)    158
Blake Walker (15)    160
Ben Mansfield (12)    161
Nellie Fraser (12)    162

## Purbrook Park School, Purbrook

Xander Harris    163
Maisy Middleton    164

## Queensbury Academy, Dunstable

Robyn Louise Sage (13)    166
Emma Pala (12)    167

## Ratton School Academy Trust, Eastbourne

Ella Molly Harris (13)    168
Billy Smith (14)    169

## Swanmore College Of Technology, Swanmore

Helen Marianne Knowles (11)    170

## The Global Academy, Hayes

Aleksandra Kraszewska (14)    172

## The Hazeley Academy, Hazeley

Ashelyn Wangui Kahoho (12)    173
Michelle Hanson (11)    174
Lily Connell (11)    176
Laia Gomez-Ortega (11)    179
Zahra Khota (12)    180
Keira Goody (11)    181
Grace Thomas (11)    182
Adam Scott (11)    183
Zenovia Kalyana (11)    184
Yaser Hameed Kadhm (11)    185
Emma Sands (11)    186
Marta Lulka (12)    187
Brandon Allun Delemere (11)    188
Gabriel Guimaraes (11)    189
Daisy Clark (11)    190
Stephanie Underhill (11)    191
Mikel Gomez-Ortega (11)    192
Mohammed Hassan Usman (12)    193
Ashton Phillips (11)    194
Olivia Shane (11)    195
Keira Lee Galloway (11)    196
Elissa Birkett (11)    197
Rhys Ingerfield (11)    198
Charlie Preston (11)    199

THE POEMS

# THE FLOWER

They love me
They love me not

The petal of loyalty
The petal of love
Though I should resist the urge
The urge of peeling off
Another petal
Showing the undesired

They love me
They love me not

Each petal is a scream
Of attention
Peeling the petals will be torture
But pleasant for them

The undesired truth
Is another step closer
To a ruined flower

They love me
They love me not

The chants of screams erupt
The look of lust from the blade
Just one more time
The thought repeating

The flower is now naked
And is broken
Tossed away...
Forgotten...

The thick scent is what is left
And the body of the flower
Along with its petals

The blade is gone now.

## Khadija Wehand (13)
Andalusia Academy, St Matthias Park

# MARION

I notice how peculiar Marion is,
As I observe its happenings blossom and wilt around me.

Milky streams reaching from its back,
A gleaming armour glazed with iron liquid,
Dancing down through Marion's tearful veins.

Through the ripple-ridden window one can see
A golden orb on the silver sea;
"Why, sweet Marion, please do tell,
Was the sky so smitten before you fell?
The stars so bright before your demise,
The canopy holding the broken girl
So glassy before the many stars?"

There is no response,
But a teasing breath on my cheek;
How so beautiful
Is Marion...

"How, dear Marion, my curiosities please do satisfy-
Do your shards of coloured hope
Split open the aching sky?
Do your green arms rise
To salute the armada of cloudy mountains
Lining Marion's flushing canvas
Where the winged darts glide,
Swimming in a creamy sky of half-light and lullaby?

Do your dark veins uncurl
To form the sweetest peach trees?"

There is no response-
But the patter of tears!

How so peculiar
Is Marion...

## Hana Abdirahman (15)
Andalusia Academy, St Matthias Park

# MY NAME

My mother gifted me my name
Something I thought was just simple and plain,
But then people started assigning me... names
Which gave me more than one simple name

To the bullies, I was 'lame'
To society, I'm just the 'same'
The people who see me, call me 'oppressed'
That apparently, I have something 'to confess'

To the people who listened to my views, I'm 'in need of a
therapist'
To people on the streets, I'm a 'terrorist'
And in the airport, I'm another 'random search'
'Cause people think I'm 'one to hurt'

But none of it's true because of the misinformation
It's hard for anyone, including myself, to deconstruct
because of the frustration
Instead of picking and individualising people, paint over a
group
Until every hijabi needs to be 'liberated' and every white is a
'racist troop'

But how can you know all this without even asking?

A person's story is self-determined
Coming out of the lips of that very person
The story is not told by the piece of cloth they decide to
wear or by melanin of their skin

It's not told by what people who look like them do, even if it's their twin

A person's story is self-proclaimed
It's nobody else's say
So before you generalise, think again
Because that's not their name.

## Khadeeja Ali (16)
Andalusia Academy, St Matthias Park

# ON THE EDGE OF HOPE

To stand on the edge,
On the cusp of a short fall to a certain death,
To remember...
Rush through the memories that pushed you to this point,
Surrounded by strangers too attached to themselves to look up,
Grasping at non-existent hope,
Trying to find a reason to stay,
Some signal,
A sign,
Hope,
To tip and sway with the breeze of unseen trains,
Then to fall like a feather,
Blown by wind of fate,
To slam against the oncoming metal slate,
Whose scratched window seems to spell out the truth you couldn't face,
Then there's me,
Lost in thoughts,
As a flash of frustration crosses my mind,
A lump of guilt rises in my throat,
Knowing that I must wait ten minutes,
As they peel off your dying body from the tracks.

## Aisha Omar (11)
Ayesha Siddiqa Girls' School, Southall

# EDUCATION STATION

Come on down to the fillin' station,
We're gonna build a generation,
How 'bout your toddler, only three,
He's gonna be an infant prodigy.
How 'bout his bro, only seven,
He's gonna do a PhD.
Tubes, tubes everywhere,
Soon you ain't be doin' childcare.
In one ear and in the other,
Just don't stress your old grandmother.
Forget the sand 'n' water,
Teach him all the things you oughta,
English, maths, science too ,
Did you know school is good for you?

Come on down to the fillin' station,
We are gonna be a generation,
Roald Dahl, Isaac Newton, Albert Einstein too,
Literature is good for you.

Come on down to the fillin' station,
What a wonderful creation,
Forget the books, what a waste of time,
Why is it that we have to learn to rhyme?
Soon this teacher will die of laughter,
For she literally is a drafter.

We would have come sooner,
However, I ain't a tuner.

## Siham Abdirahman Shire (11)
Ayesha Siddiqa Girls' School, Southall

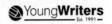

# SHOCKING MEMORIES

I awoke in a vast, empty place,
Floating unsteadily in the dark,
Hoping to meet a friendly face,
When suddenly I saw a bright spark

I started moving in the distant darkness,
When screens appeared and showed my carelessness,
The further I went, the faster I moved,
Then there came the shocking memories,
The memories I was not aware of

Everything seemed unreal, as if in a dream,
And now I regretted those memories and those with my
team,
When suddenly, my eyes turned to darkness

I woke up and found myself on the floor,
Wondering how I got down there,
But the dream,
Was it true?

## Hadia Malik (12)
Ayesha Siddiqa Girls' School, Southall

# ROBOTS, PARKS AND EVERYTHING ELSE

In the future, life won't be normal,
I don't think anything will be formal,
No parks, no parks, no barks,
No arcs, all dark,
In the future, there will be no teacher,
I don't think there will even be a creature

Robots will be normal,
Everything will be abnormal
Phones will be like water,
Life will be shorter

Because what is life without a purpose?
Things will be like a circus
Earth will be polluted,
Animals will be shooed
Future will be weird,
But will you have a beard?

**Ilhaan Wehliye (11)**
Ayesha Siddiqa Girls' School, Southall

# ON THE EDGE OF HOPE

*A lipogram without the letter C*

I live in a world full of stress,
Before I do anything, I make sure it's the best

I always feel nervous,
I wish I was fearless

And I never go to sleep,
As my mind's always going beep!

I feel the heat rising up upon me,
As if it is a swarm of buzzing bees

I never let anyone near me,
I fear that they will hate me

My home is worse,
My dad says it's just a rehearsal

Sometimes I wish I wasn't me,
But hey, this is a story between you and me.

## Sarah Wahbi (11)
Ayesha Siddiqa Girls' School, Southall

# CHANGE

The sun and wind and the beat of the sea,
All smile at me so gracefully

I run and run so carelessly,
Along great lands stretching endlessly

Everything is so free for me,
It's like the world was made for thee,
In minutes, the world begins to change,
The ground begins to shake,
Everything begins to break

Books become birds fluttering away,
A moment of silence,
Sadness,
Affray.

## Sabah Hussain (11)
Ayesha Siddiqa Girls' School, Southall

# THE HEART OF THE FOREST

I am walking in the woods,
Danger is somewhere around.
I can see all the tree roots,
And my heart is about to pound.
I reach the heart of the forest,
The trees are standing up high.
This is not a contest,
I have to look back and sigh.
To know where I am going,
I can't just spy.

## Maryama Bashir
Ayesha Siddiqa Girls' School, Southall

# THE JUNGLE

The jungle is a place,
For me to have a race

With all the bears,
And all the hares

All the animals following me,
Don't you see?

Run and run,
Have some fun

Swing on a vine,
Before there's no time

And you'll see,
How much fun you will have with me.

## Meena Hakimy (11)
Ayesha Siddiqa Girls' School, Southall

# FRIENDS!

A friend is someone we turn to when our spirits need a lift,
A friend is someone we treasure,
Because friendship is a gift.

A friend is someone who fills our lives with beauty, joy and grace,
A friend makes the world we live in,
A better and happier place.

## Mahabuba Rahman
Ayesha Siddiqa Girls' School, Southall

# THOUGHTS

*A haiku*

Is this the future?
It doesn't look like my world,
Perhaps I'm dreaming.

## Sheza Chaudry (11)
Ayesha Siddiqa Girls' School, Southall

# MAYBE

The future is grey,
For we don't know
What might be in store
In a couple of years or more

Maybe the government will reign supreme
And all the peasants will be forced to adhere,
Ministry officials sent to overthrow the Queen,
Everybody else left for worse,
They'll make us into puppets
And they'll be our masters,
Everyone will be upset
And our very old world will be covered in plasters
As people retaliate,
Men and women alike,
To give back our rights

Or maybe the Earth will decide to strike back,
Saying, "Global warming, no more of that!"
Maybe Earth will think for a while
And come to the conclusion that humans are hypocritical
and vile,
So then our world
Will nearly be fully submerged,
Only a fifth of the land that we once had
As Earth decides to strike back

Or maybe the globe is just a game,
A simulation,
Where people who're cruel
Will come to play,
To get a chance to rule the game,
We'll be forced to jump, to work and play,
We do not know who might be next

Or maybe there'll be no drink,
No alcohol to ruin lives,
No one on the street, no freezing at night,
Will the government have finally taken charge?

Build little houses and more places to work?
Our world will be a better place,
But let's not forget the wars that took place

Or maybe they'll take a different route,
A stupid man who takes the first thought that comes to
mind,
So he declares that people must only have one child,
So everyone tries to hide them away,
But great minds of siblings are killed every day,
So now it has decreased by half,
They say, "More jobs will be available, you'll be able to
work."
But many people still cry at night,
As they remember that terrible fight

Maybe we'll be able to move to Mars,
But we'll destroy that planet, the same as ours,
Maybe from hundreds of years of war,
Earth and Mars will be no more

So our future is still not clear,
It's extremely delusional
And very debatable,
But only time will tell,
Will we survive?
Will we die?
What will happen, we do not know,
But let's just hope for the best
And let go.

## Kara Coulthard (12)

Broadoak Maths & Computing College, Weston-Super-Mare

# TEENAGE YEARS

We sit up in our rooms, like prisoners awaiting jails,
Boggling our minds with silly stunts and fails
I'm not a stereotype, you see,
I'm just growing up and proud to be me

Instagram has us going, Snapchat just as well,
We pose in front of cameras, thinking we look just swell
You say that we're on too much,
Worried that we won't stay in touch
With the real world and its wonderful nature

I know not all teens are like this all the time,
It's okay to be different and so that's why
I'm writing this to tell you, you're perfect how you are,
Don't let anyone change you, be your own shooting star

Everyone is different,
That's just how it is.

## Maisie Smith (12)
Broadoak Maths & Computing College, Weston-Super-Mare

# IN THE MIND OF DAKOTA JACKSON

Dakota was smiling, but his mind was a tempest.
A raging torrent of anguish, further internalising his fear.
In the eve, his mind was a still rivulet with no fish.
No ideas or concepts, just still, serene waters.

While quiet on the surface, the uneven depths were a place no one,
Not even Dakota, would tread.
It was a daunting void,
Negated of any life,
With a distant breeze just managing to move it.
The depths were an isolated cage of unbarring emotions and fragmented memories,
Ever jaded via the long and waiting tear in Dakota's head.
As if someone had taken a piece of him,
Perhaps someone had taken it all from him.

But fish would swim again,
Swirling and making the subdued waters light up with green light.
But the fish were all dead.
Bobbing on the cold surface,
Waiting to be enveloped in the lifeless fjord at a patronising speed.

At the bottom was a creature too horrific to imagine,

It was a blinding cluster of tarnished reminisce,
Haunting Dakota and those around him.
This monster was the called The Media,
A hideous manipulator, filled with lies and malice.

This is what had killed the fish.

This hideous presence lingered in Dakota's head,
Reminding him that he was unlike the others that followed
in its course footsteps,
Allowing it to take full control over them,
Possess them,
They were its puppets
And it liked to put on a show.

## Cassandra Mae McDonnell (12)

Broadoak Maths & Computing College, Weston-Super-Mare

# THE MARK

Doors creep slowly open, like a crack, opening up to the
remains of Earth
The first shard of light for thousands of millenniums
Tentative feet, first human ones on Earth, since they left
their mark

A perfect field of green. Grass, trees and bushes
A perfect dome of grey. Light rainclouds that hover in the
sky
Masking the terror of the Mark that humanity created all
those years ago

A concrete skeleton towers above the haunted ground
Crawling with cracks, mould and the image of death
Hiding in its maze of silent hallways, the truth

A swing squeaks in the light breeze
Neglected, unused
By the very people who created it

A streetlight flickers between life and death
Starved of power
Casting a sickly orange glow over the desolate streets

All humanity created, it destroyed
Over its own green jealousy and hate
A corrupted species that can't live with each other

And now they're back

Surveying their ancestors' mistakes
Cursing them for the planet they left them with

How they took it and covered it with bruises of concrete
Slashed it with cuts of gas
Before finally, coating it with the Mark

The Nuclear Mark.

## Matthew Furlong (12)
Broadoak Maths & Computing College, Weston-Super-Mare

# THE JOURNEY TO CHRISTMAS

*Haiku poetry*

Christmas is coming
The ground is covered in snow
People are prepared

The ground is icy
This Christmas is looking white
Most are cheerful now

As parents are warm
The children are having fun
The snow is stunning

The bells are ringing
The stockings are up today
Children are happy

Christmas is coming
Closer and closer each day
The presents are wrapped

Christmas Eve is here
People are getting turkeys
The shops are like mad

All the songs are on
Children have their PJs on

And settling in bed

Finally, it's here
Presents are being unwrapped
Smiles on their faces

The turkey is here
Everyone is very pleased
And stuffing their mouths

Christmas is over
All the children are in bed
Parents are now happy.

**Daniella Barrett (13)**
Broadoak Maths & Computing College, Weston-Super-Mare

# THE FUTURE

What will happen in the future? Well, we don't know
Will there be lots and lots of snow?
Will there be jetpacks?
Or maybe you won't have to pay tax
Will half of the world be underwater?
Maybe everyone will be much shorter
Could your daily food be in a single pill?
Maybe there will be robots sent out to kill
Will people get older?
Or maybe it won't get colder
What will people do as a job?
Will there still be corn on the cob?
Will there be floating trains?
Or maybe even virtual car lanes
Will you have a flying, self-driving car?
Maybe in the real world, you are replaced with an avatar
Maybe you will have your very own robot
And everyone lives on a very big yacht?

## Mitchell Simms (12)
Broadoak Maths & Computing College, Weston-Super-Mare

# LEAVING

Life is not amusing when you leave
As you play and enjoy the days
When you leave in distress and pain
Only memories of the time will remain
When you wave bye to your friends
Your regret will never end
Memories will pass by in your mind
When they were divine

But if you feel like this, all you need to say is this:

Happiness is a relief, you will get it if you believe
It is not what you do wrong, it is what you got
If you're having a dull day, just beam a lot
And the clouds above will go away
You cannot buy happiness
Because happiness will find you
If not, life will always be blue
Happiness is free and it is waiting for you and me.

## Merlin Sony (11)
Broadoak Maths & Computing College, Weston-Super-Mare

# THE FUTURE

In the future, I predict flying cars,
Talking scooter handlebars
Self-driving aeroplanes,
Very aerodynamic

Human robots cooking for you,
Doing all the things you need to do
Doing your chores just for you,
Whilst you sit on the toilet and watch Dr Who

Flying houses will do the job,
You will take your things wherever you want
Robot postman so they do not have to get out of bed,
Now it gives them time to toast some bread

'The Hunger Games' might come alive,
You might be an avatar
How many people will travel far?

You might have your very own self-writing pen,
It would be done in a count to ten.

## Zion Cozens (12)
Broadoak Maths & Computing College, Weston-Super-Mare

# SOMETIMES

Our thoughts,
Our feelings,
Our actions,
They affect everything

Sometimes we feel sadness,
We wake up and look at our reflections,
Then we let out the rainstorm inside of us
Until our bodies are empty of its oceans

Sometimes we feel hope,
We hope that everything will get better,
That something brilliant will come upon us,
We feel as if there is a light at the end of the tunnel

Sometimes we feel excitement,
We are excited for this wonderful thing to happen,
Something that makes our hearts beat faster, faster...
Until the extravagance is over

Our thoughts,
Our feelings,
Our actions...

## Grace Atkinson (12)
Broadoak Maths & Computing College, Weston-Super-Mare

# WHAT DOES THE FUTURE HOLD?

Nobody knows of the meaning of future,
What will be our later life?

A great significance of value represents future,
Will we be dead or alive?
Nobody knows...

Can we save ourselves and the planet?

Electric cars are scarcely seen,
Saving waste is forgotten by many,
But not by those of us who demand a future

Those who beg for an after planet for future generations,
Turning off lights seems difficult to some

What's next? Robots doing everything for us?
We already have speaking machines who can play songs
and tell you the weather.
What's next? Not for us, but for the planet,
What's next?

## Faith Zaire (12)
Broadoak Maths & Computing College, Weston-Super-Mare

# THE LANDING BEACHES!

Going to beaches where the D-Day landings took place,
The place where soldiers got shot square in the face,
You can still hear the gunfire from the opposing side,
It's only a matter of seconds until another gets shot in the
eye

Seventy years later, you can still hear the dreaded
scream of fear,
Seeing friends and foes fall around you,
Is not a pretty sight to see

I'm standing on the sand that claimed back France,
From those dreaded Nazis,
"We shall fight on the beaches!"
For our country

And we will remember them,
No matter how many years have passed

We will remember them.

## Hugo Marsden (12)
Broadoak Maths & Computing College, Weston-Super-Mare

# IN MY OPINION

*Haiku poetry*

In my opinion,
Everyone needs to stop this,
All of the killing

In my opinion,
We need to put down the guns,
And stop all the hate

In my opinion,
We need to put down the knives,
We should love others

In my opinion,
No one needs to tie the noose,
We all need the love

In my opinion,
They should stop killing themselves,
And start living life

In my opinion,
No one has the right to go,
Do not overdose

In my opinion,
Do not ever try to die,
Don't do it again

In my opinion,
In my unheard opinion,
My very own thoughts.

## Phoebe Miles (12)

Broadoak Maths & Computing College, Weston-Super-Mare

# UNDER THE WATERFALL

Clambering up a staircase of rocks,
Feet squelching in waterlogged shoes,
An impatient queue of children waiting to jump.

As boys and girls hurl themselves bravely into the water,
I watch as my turn nears and I climb up to crawl beneath
the tumbling waterfall.

Underneath, the air smells sweet and there is no noise,
But the gentle stroking of drops on my helmet
which calms me.

I stand with my toes over the edge, waiting for
the signal to jump.

And it comes quicker than expected and I'm in the air,
Falling, down, down toward the turquoise lagoon,
But it feels great - like I'm free.

**Lily Duffy (12)**
Broadoak Maths & Computing College, Weston-Super-Mare

# UPHILL POEM

As I look out of my window,
I see the trees waving in the wind,
Leaves floating down to the short green grass,
People climbing up to the church,
As it waves the English flag with pride

Cows grazing on the lush green grass,
Birds perching lightly on their backs,
Beyond the church, rock climbers scale the quarry,
Arriving at their summit,
Looking out over the horizon

A dramatic change happens as night falls,
An orange flame appears on the tower,
Casting a flickering glow around and about,
As the cows settle down for the night,
In the quiet shadow beneath.

**Charlie Beal (12)**
Broadoak Maths & Computing College, Weston-Super-Mare

# WE MAY NEVER KNOW

Who knows what lies in the future?
Maybe it's teleportation,
We could travel far, too far.
Maybe it's robots,
Good or bad, they could do it all.
Maybe dogs could talk,
Who knows?

Or perhaps it's war?
Maybe creation will end,
Could it be peace?
Happiness and hope,
Could it be that we end world hunger?
Feed a nation...

We could travel further than imagination,
Go to another planet,
Meet another race,
Or aliens,
How about flying cars?
The future is full of surprises...
Who knows, what do you think?

**Max Allsopp (13)**
Broadoak Maths & Computing College, Weston-Super-Mare

# WHY?

Hurricane Florence and Hurricane Michael
Oh, what bad you've brought to the world
You have destroyed everything in your way
It's like you're on a never-ending pathway

Do you know how many people you've killed today?
You have disheartened families
Why do you do this to people?
You hurt them like a needle

Your ghastly winds destroy people's homes
You don't just destroy them on the outside
You destroy them on the inside

Just tell me why you do this to us?
Why are you this cruel?
Just leave us alone, you fool.

## Brandon Warren (12)
Broadoak Maths & Computing College, Weston-Super-Mare

# THE APOCALYPSE

It was always sunny in Sanctuary City
Until the day the big boom came
As the world plunged into darkness
And reality did the same

Nobody ventured near Wendy Point
Nobody knew what was there
Us humans fear the unknown
Yet what came after was more of a scare

I never thought nuclear power would go wrong
They told us it was all okay
We believed them blindly
And never had anything to say

And now look at us
Living like savages in the wasteland
We crafted the future
Now half of us are buried in sand.

## Lukas Harvey (12)

Broadoak Maths & Computing College, Weston-Super-Mare

# MY FIRST PET

*Haiku poetry*

My first ever pet,
A small, black Labrador pup
With a silky coat

Her petite black tail,
Her expressive, joyful eyes,
Her new, peaceful life

A well-behaved dog,
I gave her the name Willow
For her cheerful life

She slept on my bed,
Curling into a small ball
Her weight on my legs

Willow wears a big black coat,
Her coat as black as new tar
Her tail goes wag wag!

I've loved her for years,
And I'll love her for lots more
For the rest of our great lives.

## Lacey May Weston-Marlow (12)

Broadoak Maths & Computing College, Weston-Super-Mare

# THE OMINOUS CASTLE

*Haiku poetry*

There were ominous
Vibes because of the big storm
Then he almost died

He slipped and fell down
And almost hit a big spike
Somehow, he still lived

But somehow, he cracked
His head open and it spilt
A lot of red blood

The castle became
A blur to Tommy because
He was quite concussed

All of a sudden
He blacked out and when he woke
He saw men in masks

The man drew a knife
He fainted in horror, then
He never woke up.

## Will Bamsey (12)
Broadoak Maths & Computing College, Weston-Super-Mare

# ANGRY CAT

My dog hates my cat,
Because she is fat
She eats all of his food,
Which he finds very rude!

My dog is called Taz,
He hangs out with the lads
My cat is called Missy,
I give her food, she gives me kisses

Sometimes Missy gets mad,
When I say Taz is a lad
She tries to bite your feet,
When she does that, it's not neat

Every day when I get home,
I give Tazzy a bone
Then I look at the angry cat,
Who has an empty bowl on her mat.

## Joe Davies (12)
Broadoak Maths & Computing College, Weston-Super-Mare

# WILD WINTERS

It is as cold as the Arctic,
How do people live in the Antarctic?
The floor is shiny,
I bet you would glide so nicely

The rooftops are like a slide,
Go down them and you will glide
The windows are so fragile,
I bet they are so agile

It is so cold,
I bet there isn't any gold
The sky is so white,
It's such a delight

The wispy winters,
The cold gives us blisters
We have to wear our hats,
Before the cold attacks.

**Violet Wilcox (12)**
Broadoak Maths & Computing College, Weston-Super-Mare

# MY CAT

My cat,
Is no bat

But sometimes when it goes outside at night,
It might stare at you through your window and give you a fright

Sometimes my cat acts like he is in a bad mood,
But I know that he does this just so I will give him food

But there are also good things about my cat,
Sometimes he's funny and he likes to wear a hat

My cat is like a little star,
And I keep all the good thoughts of him in my lovely jar.

## Emilia Bienias (12)
Broadoak Maths & Computing College, Weston-Super-Mare

# MIRROR

Mirror mirror, on the wall,
Who's the fairest of them all?

I beg you to lie,
Please say it's me
Just for once,
Make me happy

The real world is cruel,
They say I'm a fool
So now, mirror, speak,
You can even shriek

But mirror, do you have no reply?
Do you, too, turn a blind eye?
I'm in so much misery, so much pain
I'm not understood, mirror, I'm going insane!

**Daniella Marin (12)**
Broadoak Maths & Computing College, Weston-Super-Mare

# THE FEAR OF SHADOWS

*Haiku poetry*

The dark night alone,
The shadows looming, moving,
Terror reigned tonight

Lie ominously,
The screeches of crows haunting,
The shadows took form

Creeping towards me,
Suddenly, a light broke out,
Reaching back in fear

The light had vanished,
Never returned since that night,
A weapon, weakness...

Tonight, Halloween
I lie in my bed until...
The nightmares return.

## Isobel Painter (11)
Broadoak Maths & Computing College, Weston-Super-Mare

# THE CASTLE

*Haiku poetry*

It ominously
Gathered around the
Dark, menacing house

WIthout knowing what
To do, she screamed loudly, then
An ear-splitting noise

Foreboding gates shook
And opened, what's happening?
The crows were omens

Had they come for her?
Heart pounding, spine chilling her
Had they come for her?

She gasped, had to run
Would she dare go for it?
Had it come for her?

## Ashtami Ravi (11)
Broadoak Maths & Computing College, Weston-Super-Mare

# A NEW HOME

Planet Earth was gone,
Pollution finished it,
But hope was not lost,
Mars was our home now,
We made Mars habitable,
We terraformed it,
Water made it like Earth,
It was peaceful until they came,
*Bang!* They attacked,
We said to survey them,
We were suddenly conquered,
We wouldn't survive this
They never gave up,
They were relentless now,
They would hunt us forever.

## Dawid Kucinski (13)
Broadoak Maths & Computing College, Weston-Super-Mare

# THE BUILDING OF ETERNAL TORTURE

*Haiku poetry*

Ominous feelings
Fill the air with terror, yet
No one runs away

Haunting images
Fill the minds of those who dare
To enter the door

Anyone who does
Take one step in the building
Will have no escape

They will be tortured
By the ghosts who suffered the
Same horrific fate

Only one person
Has made it out, will someone
Else escape alive?

**Elliott Price (11)**
Broadoak Maths & Computing College, Weston-Super-Mare

# THE FUTURE WORLD

There aren't any Stone Age people,
Or wooden carts
Nothing is broken,
No left out parts

The sun is getting hotter,
The winter's getting wetter
The storms are very windy,
Panic in the air
The world is going to end,
Disaster everywhere

We now have flying cars,
That's how we get around
They go really fast,
And don't make a sound!

**Ben White (12)**
Broadoak Maths & Computing College, Weston-Super-Mare

# THE BEAST

*Haiku poetry*

It was ominous,
The creepy creature moved in,
Around the old house

It ominously
Moved around the castle wall
And took over it

Then the castle fell
Over to it as it had
Enough power for

The castle to be
Under its reign to help and
Stop the bad omen

And then it had gone,
Set off one day, hoping to
Return to its throne.

## Romeo Immanuel (11)
Broadoak Maths & Computing College, Weston-Super-Mare

# SCHOOL TIME

*Haiku poetry*

Just think about school,
You might think that school is fun,
When others think not

Some might think it's long,
Some have opinions for school,
Some might think it's short

First day at school,
Some might not like it that much,
Some kids might like it

End of the school year,
Some might not like it that much,
Some kids might like it.

## Michael Veal (12)

Broadoak Maths & Computing College, Weston-Super-Mare

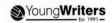

# NATURE AND WHAT YOU FIND

Juicy, green apples,
Falling down brown, rusty trees,
Ripe, ready to eat

Standing tall above us,
In their strong, majestic form,
A tree is its name

Products of oak trees,
Their children are their acorns,
Trees will develop

Every tree's strands of hair,
Connected via slender stems,
They're formed to just fall.

## Alex Roberts (12)
Broadoak Maths & Computing College, Weston-Super-Mare

# UPHILL

The church stands tall and proud,
On the hill, looking down
On all the houses glowing with
Happiness

Kites flying joyfully in the wind,
Children running through long grass
And
Wild flowers

Pubs light up with cheers and excitement,
Ice creams melt in café windows,
Children walk past, wishing they could have one.

**Charlie Deane (12)**
Broadoak Maths & Computing College, Weston-Super-Mare

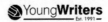
# THE MAZE

Into the maze I go,
Hedges rise sky high
New paths on every turn I take,
Dead ends on every turn I take

End,
End,
End

I'm stuck in this torturous maze

Finally, I see a way free,
Run,
Run,
Run

I'm finally free,
But of course
This wasn't the exit,
I escaped through the entrance.

**Billy Frise (12)**
Broadoak Maths & Computing College, Weston-Super-Mare

# THE OLD GRAVEYARD

*Haiku poetry*

The castle gives an
Ominous feeling as I
Walk past the great dark

Graveyard with the smell
Of bodies ominously
Creeping up my nose

The sky rumbles as
I take a step towards the
Door and *crash!* A sheep

Lies there on the grass
All burnt and dead, creepily
The door creaked open...

## Connor Grant Fieldhouse (11)
Broadoak Maths & Computing College, Weston-Super-Mare

# THE NOT-SO-AMAZING ADVENTURE

I'm going on an adventure,
Up to the mountaintop
I'm thinking of how to get there,
Should I run, walk or hop?

I'm wearing my helmet, boots and gloves,
My harness fastened on
I'm looking up towards the doves,
Oh no, my crampon fell off!

H
E
L
P!

**Jasmine Whitfield (12)**
Broadoak Maths & Computing College, Weston-Super-Mare

# CREEPY CASTLES

*Haiku poetry*

Those castles were weird
So, so menacing
I wouldn't go there

The ominous sky
That was so malevolent
Menacing it was

It was a castle
Possibly haunted and that's
How it creeped me out

You just never know
Creepily running to you
Looming scarily.

## Alexander Matthew Gronland (12)

Broadoak Maths & Computing College, Weston-Super-Mare

# THE STORM IS COMING

The storm is coming,
Time to get running,
The thundercloud is coming

The city is dark,
Not a single spark,
Dogs bark

Thunder crashes,
The lightning flashes,
The waves start bashing

The people are hiding,
The children are crying,
The storm is coming.

**James Matthew Jarvis (12) & Oskar**
Broadoak Maths & Computing College, Weston-Super-Mare

# DEADLY PLAN

*Haiku poetry*

He ominously
Disappeared into a
Flash of creepy light

Never to be seen
Again until one evil
Mysterious day

When a bunch of black
And scouring crows come and meet
At the ominous

Eye of the storm to
Create a devious plan to
Take over the world.

## Hollie Louise Hughes (11)
Broadoak Maths & Computing College, Weston-Super-Mare

# FEELINGS

Sometimes you are sad,
But usually excited,
Feelings change like mad

Happiness, sadness,
Sometimes even cautionless!
Calm and also carefulness

For a while you feel rad,
But next minute, you could feel mad!
Although it can be annoying,
We are often glad.

## Kiran Johal (12)
Broadoak Maths & Computing College, Weston-Super-Mare

# THE BAD OMEN

*Haiku poetry*

It ominously
Got greyer and greyer, *bang!*
Thunder and lightning

"Everybody, run!"
Shouted the king, "Get the kids!"
They did not hear him

It was an omen,
If- *bang!* Lightning struck tonight,
Would they all survive?

## Tyler Roan Al Bridges (11)
Broadoak Maths & Computing College, Weston-Super-Mare

# THE HURRICANE

The horrible hurricane approaches
Without a care in the world
Some people hide
And some ask why
A storm of this size
Will fall from the sky
Rain pounds
Trees will fall
But the most important thing of all
Stay safe
And evacuate.

## Jacob Palmer (13)
Broadoak Maths & Computing College, Weston-Super-Mare

# THE FUTURE

The future is fantastic,
No more racism,
No more war,
No more poor people

There are flying cars
And things are fun
Everything is different
And advanced,
Aliens are not discovered.

**Bailey Cameron Surry (12)**
Broadoak Maths & Computing College, Weston-Super-Mare

# THE LETTER

**T** he letter you sent me
**H** ad horrible thoughts
**E** ven though we never speak

**L** et me please see you again
**E** very day you ignore me
**T** he day you didn't talk to me
**T** hat was the day I thought you hated me
**E** ven though I thought we were friends
**R** eally, you could have spoken to me

**Y** ou need to speak to me again
**O** therwise, we will forget all the good times together
**U** ltimately, you are my best brother

**S** eriously, we need to be the best of friends
**E** ven though you are always with your friends
**N** ow you know how I want to speak to you, we should see
**T** hat we are friends and family.

## Skye Manley (12)
Buckler's Mead Academy, Yeovil

# THE DEEP, DARK CAVE

In the middle of nowhere
Sat in the deepest, darkest cave
A scaly, dark dragon lurked
When two daredevil humans called Tim and Dave
Went hunting for this creature on this spooky day
The dragon's claws were as sharp as a sword
Its teeth could snap any building in half
Oh, but there was more
Its nostrils flared with aggression, its wings flapped with strength
Its tail swung with pride, for this dragon was no coward
It was clear this dragon was filled with power
"Maybe we overthought this," said Dave
"Definitely," said Tim as they ran away.

## Kai Jackson (12)
Buckler's Mead Academy, Yeovil

# JUST TALK TO ME

J ust listen at least
U sed to love me
S top ignoring me
T alk to me

T alk to your beloved family
A ll you do is hide in your room
L isten to the people who love you
K ind of making me hate you

T his needs to change
O therwise we won't know you anymore

M um and Dad say they love you
E veryone misses you, the old you.

**Erin Tanswell (12)**
Buckler's Mead Academy, Yeovil

# MY WINTER AVENTURE

**W** hile I run in the roaring wind
**I** push through the snowy trees
**N** ot thinking about the pack of wolves
**T** hree of them with huge teeth
**E** ntering the forest miles from town
**R** esting behind a tree, hiding from them

**W** olves are howling around me
**O** blivious of where they are
**L** eaving as the snow falls
**F** reezing as I start to see the village.

## Jamie-Leigh Rose (12)
Buckler's Mead Academy, Yeovil

# PERFECT AS YOU

It all starts with emotional breakdowns
When you feel you aren't perfect
Or good enough for the world
And you have to be like everyone else
But that doesn't matter
If you're yourself
You'll be loved by everyone
And the people that don't like that
Are jealous of your personality and beauty
No matter how big or small
You're perfect as you.

**Georgia Feast (12)**
Buckler's Mead Academy, Yeovil

# PEOPLE'S VERSIONS

People have a version of us,
That we are a certain way,
Even though we're not,
They imagine this perfect version of us,
Judge us for who we are,
We are our own people,
Should feel comfortable in our own skin,
We can't hide ourselves,
No matter what language you use,
Race you are,
Religion you are,
We are all human.

**Lily Rose Taylor (12)**
Buckler's Mead Academy, Yeovil

# YEOVIL

*Haiku poetry*

I live in Yeovil,
Sometimes it has bad weather,
But there can be sun

It is a nice place,
There is a lot of action,
It has attractions

There are lots of shops,
To get everything you need,
Clothing to gaming

There are lots of schools,
For lots of education,
And there is lots more.

**Noah Brian Vince (13)**
Buckler's Mead Academy, Yeovil

# CHRISTOPHER

My dear friend,
Remember the days
We used to laugh and play
After days would go by day by day
I'll always remember you, bro
After I pray and pray for you
To come back
When you left my life, my fun was done
The day you went felt like the world was ending for me
I miss you.

## Josh Dey (12)
Buckler's Mead Academy, Yeovil

# WHY?

*Boom, boom, boom!*
It never stops,
Waiting for another one to come,
First in Manchester,
Then in London,
Killing themselves,
Or trying to kill others,
Never knowing where it will happen next,
Coming out of planes,
Or in person,
Bombing, why do it?

## Brooke Williams (12)
Buckler's Mead Academy, Yeovil

# DREAM-LIKE BEACH

The sun cast a tangerine glow,
The ocean-blue waves crashed on the shore,
Creating patterns like you've never seen before,
Sun-hot sand lay flat on the surface,
Seashells randomly placed across the dream-like beach,
Castles decorated with these shells places carefully.

## Connie Dopson (12)
Buckler's Mead Academy, Yeovil

# WIND

Hear it, feel it,
But it's never in sight,
Through the leaves on a tree,
The noise is calming,
But it's never in sight,
What would it be like to see the wind?
What's the colour or shape?
But it's never in sight.

## Cody Isaacs (13)
Buckler's Mead Academy, Yeovil

# ADVENTURE

We are going on an adventure,
We are going to the moon,
We are going on a boat that is blue,
We are going to use a map that tells us where to go,
The moon is like a banana sitting in a bowl.

## Charlotte Sarah Chant (12)
Buckler's Mead Academy, Yeovil

# YEOVIL

**Y** eovil is good
**E** ntertaining and fun
**O** bliterating your boredom
**V** ery good for education
**I** t has lots of shops
**L** ots of treats in store for you.

## Ethan John Atkins (12)
Buckler's Mead Academy, Yeovil

# IN THE FUTURE

Robots doing everything for you,
Robots going to school for you,
Robots taking care of you,
Vehicles hovering instead of driving on roads,
This is the future.

**Erin Lillia Parsons (12)**
Buckler's Mead Academy, Yeovil

# THE CIRCLE OF LIFE

I walk across the line of life,
Each step more cautious than the last
Discovering my future,
Picking up the pieces of the past

A toddler
A pitter-patter down the halls,
A joyous laugh echoes off the walls
Cradled in my mother's arms,
I sit there, content and calm

A child
Running through the field of flowers,
On my way to school
With my sequin pencil case,
I thought I looked so cool!
Trading things at lunchtime,
An apple for a pear
I can't wait till adulthood,
In fact, I'll see you there!

Being an adult
A thing I once looked forward to,
Turned against me in a clap
I've lost all of my sleep and I'll never get it back,
I wish I had a time machine
To turn back all the clocks,

To take away this stress and strife
To make it all just stop.

And so just like this life, my friend,
This poem too shall sadly end
Although, a wise old man once said,
"Your life isn't over when you're dead."

## Layla Mburu (11)
Chiltern Academy, 1-9

# NEW HOME, NEW LIFE

A new life and a new beginning,
A chance to enjoy brand new winnings
Kind-looking faces,
With brand new places

Hugs and kisses to say goodbye,
This was all happening within a blink of an eye
Returning the key back to the owner,
Made me feel like such a loner

All I could do now was hope,
Hope for the best but it was hard to cope
I thought of sleeping in a new house,
It wasn't just going to be a brick house

There was just no proof,
That I was moving into a good roof
Were the people nice?
Or were they as cold as ice?

I thought of leaving precious people with tears,
All I could say to them was, "Cheers!"
They helped me throughout,
With no doubt

Out we go through the door,
The tears had made my eyes feel sore
Maybe if I had a good rest,

Then moving may be the best

Well now here I am,
This was surely no scam
This leaves me to a good ending,
To me, the money was definitely worth spending.

### Saadia Naser (11)

Chiltern Academy, 1-9

# THE BILLOWING SEA GIANT

A blanket of blue,
With white clouds too
The sun blazes down,
Over the whole town

The ripples suddenly tower overhead,
It makes people's eyes fill with dread
They are scuttling as fast as a centipede,
But they are no match with its speed

Piercing cries of horror,
People's hearts fill with terror
The billowing sea giant towers over them all,
Making them seem so small

Still, its fury hasn't cooled down,
After flooding the whole town
Its pounding waves lash against the buildings wildly,
Crushing them down very easily

Finally, the giant calms down,
Making the whole town frown
One day, it will wake up again,
Causing more destruction and pain

The giant is back in his deep sleep,
Leaving the adults and the children to weep
The whole town has changed into a mess,
What will happen next, can you guess?

## Sreesha Sri Ramoju (12)
Chiltern Academy, 1-9

# PRIMARY SCHOOL LIFE

We'll sign our shirts and hug our friends,
As we know it's not really the end
We hope you'll let us visit someday,
As we'll miss you in all different ways
So thank you, WAJS, for all you've done,
The memories have been of smiles and fun
You've been great, that's what we say,
And for all your help, we're giving an A!
On second thoughts, that's not really enough
From all Year 6, let's give an A+!
Now that we're leaving, we'll say how we feel,
Our heartfelt thanks are deeply real
You've made learning fun and helped us see,
That all our lessons are valuable
You encouraged our efforts and guided us too,
Believed in us like our parents do
Some lessons were a challenge, others were the best,
Projects put Mum and Dad to the test!
We now much leave our childhood site,
For time moves on and the time is right.

**Labib Khan (11)**
Chiltern Academy, 1-9

# GONE

I came in the house and there wasn't a sound,
I looked up and down and all around

I closed my eyes because I thought it was a dream,
But when I opened them, it was just obscene

"What's this red thing on the floor?
Oh, wait! It's all over the door!"

In the corner of my eye, I saw something there,
It looked so silky, like my mum's hair

I went over there to check it out,
But it was my family without a doubt

Tears slowly dripped down my face,
It was seriously such a big disgrace

Every day I mourn how I lost them,
Especially how big it cost them

Now I'm in this world all alone,
But I've seriously grown as I'm living on my own

But when they look down to me, I hope they remember,
How I felt when I lost them in December.

**Kumayl Abbas Naqvi (11)**
Chiltern Academy, 1-9

# WHY?

I wasn't sure
What went wrong?
Then the worst thing happened
That changed my life not so long ago

I wish I could've seen you
One last time
Before you had to say goodbye
At that moment, my heart shattered

As I grew older, years passed
I started forgetting about you
I was happy that moment didn't last
Because then the truth was revealed

Living without you was tricky
I stayed strong, I didn't cry
But my heart slowly started to heal
When I finally met you

The happiest moment of my life occurred
I hugged you and you hugged me
Wishing that we would never let go

I was so thankful my mom cared for me
All those years, she worked hard
Just to keep me happy

I hope to see you again
Someday in July.

## Christiana Arsine (11)
Chiltern Academy, 1-9

# CHANGE

Losing my friend felt like the end
Please just come back to make our amends
I have a question, where did I go wrong?
You said, "Forever," but forever's not long
We had a story, you've begun a new chapter
Without you, there's no laughter
It was supposed to be just you and me against the world
It's now just you and the other girls
I've tried to be strong, I've tried to be tough
I wasn't good for you, I wasn't enough
They treated you badly, shooed you like a bag covered
in dirt
I came to help you because you were hurt
We're not friends, nor are we enemies
We are sisters, against all the deadly
After you left, although it was strange
I'm glad you came back, it's been a great change.

**Meriem Hammoun (12)**
Chiltern Academy, 1-9

# EDUCATION FOR A BETTER TRANSFORMATION

I started high school,
To avoid being a fool
Even though some people thought it wasn't cool,
But it gave me the right tools

I started education,
Though I'd rather be on vacation
But I wanted to excel and thrive,
As well as trying to strive

I started education,
For a new transformation
This was just a formation,
But it felt like I was in a new generation

I started high school,
Then I thought I was fooled
But it was pretty cool
Even though it didn't really rule

My first day went well,
Well, that's what people could tell
Though they didn't yell,
But I still stood with my feet glued like gel.

**Haleema Naeem (11)**
Chiltern Academy, 1-9

# FOREST ADVENTURE

One beautiful, star-filled night,
I saw a magnificent sight
Under the blue moon, there was a fox
With nice brown locks
I realised this was a test
While watching a bird build its nest
I was bewildered by what I found,
A little baby bird on the ground
I went and put it in the tree,
Then I fell and cut my knee
I went searching for a remedy,
Then I saw a snail up high
I climbed and when I reached the snail, I saw it was a lie,
Then descending upon me was a mist
I didn't get the gist,
I walked and thought about what a night it'd been
I couldn't believe what I had seen,
I emerged from the mist and saw my home
Home sweet home.

## Aadam Mohammed Imran (11)

Chiltern Academy, 1-9

# CHANGE

Changes come both big and small,
But without them, we can't live at all,
Change is the thing that makes us grow,
Just like the sun turns into snow,

Some of these changes affect every day,
Things that change you in every single way,
Every hour, every minute, you think about it,
And then you realise you can't live without it,

What if I change, what if you change?
The question is...
What if it doesn't?

If nothing ever changed, you wouldn't know,
You'd never think and you'd never grow,
So just think about change, it's all around you,
It's amazing, change, it will astound you.

## Ashantia Marie Fearon (11)
Chiltern Academy, 1-9

# CHANGE

Change is something we all go through,
It will appear to be slightly new to you
No matter what age we all go through it,
We can't sit there and just quit
You never know, you might have some fun,
Well come on, your journey has just begun

From time to time, things can be boring,
But you haven't tried everything so why not go exploring?
You have to remember, never doubt yourself,
Don't hide behind someone, just say, "I am myself!"
Never give up, try your hardest,
Just for you, you are the largest

Be yourself and never change,
Because there's no one out there who is the same.

**Amilia Gillas (11)**
Chiltern Academy, 1-9

# ODE TO CHANGE

Change is like the seasons
The colder months are hard
The warmer months are easy
The seasons have lots in store for us
Just as much as the future
Maybe those simple changes
Are as bad as those hard ones
Maybe we don't notice it
Maybe we are blind to changes
We should open our eyes
To view the beauty of the changes
Oh change, the things you bring
Oh change, the things you take
I can't wait to see things you'll take
And what you'll bring
Why, change, bring me good
Take away my troubles
Change, you help me live
Change, oh how I love you so much.

## Isabella Lismanis (11)
Chiltern Academy, 1-9

# OH CAKE!

Cake, oh cake
You and me would make a great date,
There's something that I just can't take...
The way you just sit there all cakey and nice,
Behind the counter
At a dangerously affordable price,
Oh cake
What am I going to do?
I came in for a sandwich,
But now there is you!
How am I going to fix this awful dilemma?
Unless I eat the cake and put the blame on my sister, Ella
I can't take this anymore!
Oops!
And now you're gone,
In my tummy
There's something you should know,
Oh, cake
You had me at hello!

## Krystal Kankonde (11)
Chiltern Academy, 1-9

# MY IMAGINATION

I put in the silver, shining and sparkling box,
The fur of the strong and murderous tiger,
A glass of water from an ocean in South Korea,
Or a scream from a person...

I put in the shimmering box,
The objects from the ancient times,
The lightning and thunder,
Piercing and blasting,
*Roar!*
Or the sense of hilarious humour.

I put in the silver box,
Gold and silver coins,
All the cash from all the banks in the world,
Or have a cash tree growing every minute
And a howl from the silver-black wolf with golden eyes...

**Muhammad Riyadh Hamid (11)**
Chiltern Academy, 1-9

# 24 WEEKS AND 5 DAYS

We all thought she'd have a miserable life,
Just because she nearly died
The whole family was at the hospital day and night,
Whilst me and my brother were having a fight
Born as big as my mum's palm,
Now life is calm
Until she's climbing out the window,
Pretending she's a hero
Now every year on the day she was born,
We give massive cakes till they're all gone
ROP, CLD, ADHA to name a few,
When she's in bed, my mum sighs, "Phew!"
El-Hania is this girl's name,
Even the doctors proudly acclaim.

## Maryam Rezzag-Lebza (11)
Chiltern Academy, 1-9

# CHANGE

This year's poetry day theme is change,
Some people may find it daunting but it's easy to gauge
There are changes happening every day,
Some may be harder than others to say

Poems can have many different meanings,
Possible adventure, but sometimes stealing
Some make you start crying,
Others can make you start jeering

Poems can bring out a lot of emotions,
Tears streaming down your face, creating oceans
They can also bring out a lot of joy,
Like pirate stories with Captain Hook, ahoy!

**Zain Shan (11)**
Chiltern Academy, 1-9

# CHANGING IS UNSTOPPABLE

People say we only live once, I don't believe it's true,
As we become different people depending on what we go
through

From the day we arrive on Earth we develop, grow and
change,
So how do we remain as one when nothing stays the same?

I think it's us when we're using magic powers without us
even realising,
If so, why isn't there something called shrinking?

Yesterday you have gone away, but don't cry for her,
As you are who you are today, that was just the little girl
you were...

**Tanisha Chowdhury (12)**
Chiltern Academy, 1-9

# THE BEGINNING OF THE LAST DEATH

With bloodstains on the floor
I felt like someone was watching me from the door
My breath stuck in my throat
I ran and escaped into a dreadful, broken boat
They splashed icy water in my face
Off I floated through the land
Then I felt a cold hand
I turned to see my ghostly dead love
And the one I was to marry
But I was taken under
I thrashed and tried to push myself
Towards the surface of the waters
I drowned into the bed of darkness
And this may be the cost of my foolishness.

## Hasan Mahmud Chowdhury (11)
Chiltern Academy, 1-9

# MY DADAZI (GRANDPA)

Oh, how much I miss you,
I think about you all night
You always told me what to do,
Because you were always right

I live in darkness now,
Because you were my only light
I struggle all day, I have no might,
My life was all colourful
But now it's black and white

I don't understand
Why you had to go,
My life was flying high
Now it has hit an all-time low

I try to remember you,
But I have nothing to show,
Now my life is full of woe.

**Mariyah Naser (11)**
Chiltern Academy, 1-9

# A GLORIOUS SOLDIER

A poem for one lost,
A general with no cost
For you lie in our heart,
A new generation we will start
As we call out your name,
We pay you no blame,
For England gives you a standing ovation

With high spirits, we pass the torch,
Our sadness is left to scorch
Our nation will celebrate your glory
The youth will remember your story
Your families will recover from the sorrow,
Their hope will renew tomorrow

We will remember them.

## Cleopatra Attah (12)
Chiltern Academy, 1-9

# WEATHER IS A FUNNY THING

The change that happens every day,
Is the fact of the weather change
Whatever the weather, we have it anyway,
Weather is good, is bad, is strange

It's freezing, it's boiling,
It's sunny or grey
It's snowing, it's raining,
It's blowing trees away

So be prepared, you never know,
Once it's snowing and it will carry on
The next day is sunny, wow, what a surprise,
So hurry up, don't wait for the ice!

**Emilia Weronika Nizankowska (11)**
Chiltern Academy, 1-9

# CHANGE DOESN'T HAVE TO BE A NIGHTMARE

When my ears heard the news
I was shocked,
I didn't know what to do
To be thankful or heartbroken?
No emotion
Could describe what I felt inside,
I didn't want a new baby
To steal my spotlight

But soon I learnt,
She wasn't so bad
She was kinda cute,
I had to face the facts

And now I know,
Change doesn't have to be a nightmare
Instead,
It brought my family together.

**Tasmiyah Chowdhury (11)**
Chiltern Academy, 1-9

# MY WORST NIGHTMARE

My worst nightmare
Gives me chills throughout the night

My worst nightmare
Makes me shiver in defeat

My worst nightmare
Makes me soak in sweat

My worst nightmare
Causes me to panic and despair

But when my eyes open
I no longer tremble with fear

I realise I've just conquered
My worst nightmare.

**Makayda Williams (11)**
Chiltern Academy, 1-9

# CHANGES

Changes can be good,
Changes can be bad
They can show you something,
You thought you never had

People move on,
Leave your world behind,
Although you can't feel it,
They're always on your mind

When they leave you,
Don't be sad
You'll make new friends,
The best you've ever had!

**Lauren Gibson (11)**
Chiltern Academy, 1-9

# LIVING THE PAST AND FUTURE

Life is rough in the past
But in the future, it's fast
Changes happen in the future
But living on has changed our culture
It has changed everything within a hole
But not who we are within our soul
The thing we should not forget
Live your life, great and divine
Don't let bad mates upon your spine.

**Matthew Orisakwe (11)**
Chiltern Academy, 1-9

# THE PEN

I am the pen that gave you notes,
I am the notes that gave you an education,
I am the education that gave you a job,
I am the job that gave you money,
I am the money to buy a new pen.

**Rayann Chalouache (11)**
Chiltern Academy, 1-9

# MOURNING

Sweetest tranquility and break of dawn,
Over the last night, we mourn.
Weeping softly, not depressed for what we have lost,
But for the agony of the mental line we crossed.
To wake as solemn as a mourning mother,
The wake of a far from seldom morning shudder.
We gather thoughts and collect borrowed words,
And borrow a smile from our muscles to hide the morning
hurt.
To wish to sleep forever more,
But wish to escape the escape of the night-time fall.
The double standards of depressed best friends,
Create loving arguments that meet no ends.
As we strive to convince others of what we see in them,
But deny others of what they see in us, proclaiming that we
will not mend.
Bitter tears cast that died at the grave of the sun,
Accumulated as tears cast in hearts at the grave sight of
another's dead son.
Knowing the truth but acting on lies,
Feeding ourselves lines of our flesh meant for flies.
Sweetly caressing our loved with love,
And harshly stabbing our hated selves with the opposite of,
Your silhouette hanging,
Your head-turned gun banging;
The slit of your wrist,

And drowning of all of you to exist;
Is nothing but a common sight.
The plagued possessed screaming, bleeding tar that is your mind
Envelops you in the night.
A yearning for perfection but a bittersweet addiction of the broken.
You would rather lie charred than let your mind be open.

## Mia Kenny (14)
Harlington Upper School, Harlington

# THE ISSUE OF OUR SOCIETY

Trapped, trapped in my head,
Where there's nowhere to go,
Nowhere to hide

Trapped, trapped in my head,
Where no words are said,
Trapped in an unresponding body

Words, trapped in my mouth,
The only things escaping are mumbles and grumbles
I'm trapped

My body is a trap,
One I have sprung,
And all that I am, is trapped inside

I'm trapped, trapped in my head,
Where there's nowhere to go,
Nowhere to hide

I beg them to help,
I beg them to see,
To see the real me

But I'm trapped,
Trapped in a world with words only
Coming out on screens,

Where they're everywhere

There is nowhere you can go,
There is nowhere you can hide
We're all trapped,
Trapped in an unresponsive society.

**Abbie Louise Giles (15)**
Harlington Upper School, Harlington

# DEAR MUM, YOU WERE RIGHT

Mum, you were right
One week into sixth form
It is different
Sorry, I've been busy
My best friend and I
Haven't spoken in a week
But it's okay
I've been busy

My stutter is back
I think it's because my hands are always shaking
My mind is my only friend
And she never stops talking
So it's okay
I've been busy

I was alone
But I learnt to turn lonely into angry
Now angry is busy
So when I say I've been busy
I mean I've been eating in the library
To avoid confronting the empty side of the bench

I don't really sleep
I'm comforted by the dark

But I do fear the days
Because they are living nightmares

Mum, I *am* lonely.

## Isabelle Brown (16)
Harlington Upper School, Harlington

# IT

It takes control of what was once innocence,
It burns innocence,
It changes innocence,
It is in every war made by man

It is in every single cold, breathless day,
It is in every life you cannot pray,
It is in the nightmare you fear the most,
It will make you feel alone

It will poison your mind,
It loves to burn innocence,
It will hurt you,
It is invincible

It is everywhere,
It is death.

**Aoife Murphy (14)**
Harlington Upper School, Harlington

# BLOOD

A split-second decision
A punch
A stab
He falls
I dash
A siren
A flash
I hide
Escape
But I can't
Erase
The blood on my hands
Blood on my hands
Blood on my hands.

## Michelle Danga (14)
Harlington Upper School, Harlington

# SILENCE

Silence,
A gunshot,
A scream,
A crowd,
A loved one down,
A siren,
Blue lights,
Tears shed for the lost,
Thoughts and prayers,
Silence.

**Daisy Webb (14)**
Harlington Upper School, Harlington

# ALONE IN THE CLOUDS

I sit here all day as you fantasise about the person I'm not
Every time we speak, it hits me like a gunshot
For I am not the girl you once fell for
If you don't want me in your life, I'll open the door
As you take your path into another one's life
I'll sit here alone and keep on twisting the knife
For my once-loved heart has been ripped in two
And my qualities in life have become very few
Do you know what it feels like when nobody's there?
It's like a blade to the heart making a very deep tear
So you go off and live your dream
And say goodbye to our one-made team
For it isn't called love if you're not prepared to chase
I've been running too long and Earth is no longer my happy place
I know sometimes it can get real rough
But each fight you fight, you'll get more tough
I ask you not to throw your life away
Tomorrow could always be a brighter day
Don't waste your time on this floating rock
Find one person, not a flock
So when the sun sets after each day
Remember that one's life is taken against their say
But don't you throw your life away
Just 'cause you're not loved by a few crowds
As one day, child, you'll be high above these clouds...

## Lisa Duke (12)
Hawley Hurst School, Blackwater

# I WISH I HAD NEVER MET HER

I wish I had never met her
I regret all the time we spent together
Everything I did for her
Her personality, everything, it's different
I won't forgive her, ever
For what she has done
I feel my insides rot, she hurt me a lot
Rage, anger boiling inside of me
Trying to erupt
Like a fierce volcano

She's changed
She's trying to be someone she's not
I don't like it, it's not her
She's not herself, she's unfamiliar

Nothing can replace the hole in my heart
The feeling of emptiness
Feeling like I am alone
Missing a part of my heart
The pain, the trust
The trust that rotted away, day after day
Thinking about her hurts

I can feel the strain in my heart just typing this

It burns, I can feel the empty space she left
Nothing can ever replace the hole she left
Despite how much I want someone to refill it
I don't want this hole that never ends

I don't know what I feel
Sometimes frustration, sometimes emptiness

I don't want to admit it,
But I miss her a lot
I miss the friendship we built over those years
Everything we went through together
And I know she misses me too
I can see it in her face
But now it's over
And she's never coming back.

**Amelie King (13)**
Hawley Hurst School, Blackwater

# THE SACRED SWORD

It fell from the sky, into the jungle,
In my eyes, I could see it shine
I ran to the jungle and to my surprise,
I saw a boy standing shy

There was an underground mine,
It didn't look fine
It was a cold, dark place with no one around,
As I was going down, there was not a single sound

I went down and saw a deep hole,
I didn't go further down because it was not my role
I just travelled further down the mine,
And everything else seemed fine

As I travelled deeper, I finally saw a glowing light,
So I went towards it with a shivering fright
As I got further, I heard breathing
I turned to my right and saw a human being

He went and pulled the sword but then fell down,
All of a sudden, I turned around and found the whole town
Everyone came to see what had happened here,
When they saw him fall, they all trembled in fear

I was brave and pulled the sword, I didn't fall,
I turned around looking very tall
Everyone was shocked,

As the sword was in my hand
And no longer in the rock.

## Aryan Patel (12)
Hawley Hurst School, Blackwater

# I'M GONE

Can they not see this smile I am faking?
Can they not see my heart slowly breaking?
They ask me, "Are you okay?" whenever I'm down,
Yet, I still know that they can't see me drown

Soon, I'll be forgotten deep under the ground,
But the world will keep moving round and round
People keep growing, people move on,
I feel so alive, even though I'm gone

He said he loved me and that he cared,
But then he left me and my heart completely teared
I lived all alone with no one all these years,
And now my eyes are closed, I've finally dried my tears

I've finally got the freedom that I'd always yearned for,
He kept taunting me, haunting me until my ears became
sore
Now that I'm liberated, I can start breathing,
Even though my heart is dead, it still seems to be beating

Can they not see my tears rolling down?
Of course they can't, because all I do is frown
I cry so much but only on the inside,
"Life is great!" but you know I lied.

## Siya Sardar (12)
Hawley Hurst School, Blackwater

# THE HEART BATTLE

My feelings had changed a lot over time,
Little did I know, so had my best friend's
During a lesson of biology, all the secrets spilt,
Turned out we both liked the same guy

I'm very sure that her heart shattered in that moment,
I looked into her eyes and had regretted saying anything
From that moment on,
I felt like I had mildly lost my best friend to a boy

When we went home that day,
The most random thought crossed our minds
A lyric prank is what we thought of,
I had to send love-like messages to this guy

Then I got responses and you will never guess,
This boy actually liked me back since January
Both of our hearts shattered in that second,
I felt like the most evil person alive

Now me and him are the closest of friends,
My best friend and I have made amends
I'm wishing this battle to go to bed,
The heart battle now ends.

## Vidhita Walia (12)
Hawley Hurst School, Blackwater

# THE FUTURE

What does the future hold?
Where will it take us?
Will our cars be on the road?
Will our cars be in the sky?
Will there even be roads?
Will there even be cars?

Will there be restaurants?
How will we eat?
Will it be fresh?
Will it be frozen?
Or will it be a meal in a pill?

Will our towns and cities be crowded?
Will we live in floating houses?
Will it be clean or will it be dirty?
Will we be happy or will we be sad?

What will happen to our animals?
Will there be green fields and sunshine?
Will we have pets and parks to walk them in?
What will happen to our wildlife and will they become extinct?

Will we still have mobile phones and computers?
Or will we have chips implanted in our bodies?
Will we have the Internet and satellite dishes?

Or will we have intergalactic Internet?

Will robots rule the world?

**Joshua Brooks (12)**
Hawley Hurst School, Blackwater

# BROKEN

I'm told to stay quiet as my lips are only for kissing,
I'm told to not be hurt by the words you're hissing
But I'm tired of living like my life is in your hands,
No path, no direction, just simply your plans
I don't need you to fill the empty parts of me,
Life's not worth living if I am not free
And the poison in your heart makes you callous and cruel,
But there's no point in fire if there's no fuel
And I'm not some figure you can mold with clay,
'Cause if you can actually look past your shades of grey
You'll see I'm not just a shape,
Or something you can silence with tape
I'm a human with a heart,
Not some other person to play the part
But my struggles are my own,
Not something that can be thrown
And I'm sorry!
Sorry I'm not good enough for you,
But I love me and you should too.

**Layla Aykac (13)**
Hawley Hurst School, Blackwater

# COLOURS

What is racism?
Hurt, hate, blame and prejudice,
Judging people because of the colour of their skin is silly,
It's like saying people with long hair are bad,
Or saying people with certain names are wrong.

How can anyone be wrong or right,
When we are all different?
Black and white people don't choose their colour,
It's just nature,
Martin Luther King is a great example of fighting against racism,
He stood up for what he believed in
And improved life for all black people.

Forcing people with black skin to do jobs is also disgusting,
Because no human should be treated like that;
We are all unique individuals
And should have the same opportunities,
The colour of your skin doesn't mean anything,
We are all equal!

What is racism?
Hurt, hate, blame and prejudice,
It needs to stop.

## Violet Marie Stokes (12)
Hawley Hurst School, Blackwater

# LET'S GO

Let's go, why not?
There are a million things to explore out there
Who knows what we will find?
The limits, you say? Oh, there're none of those!
The world is an open door
And all you have to do is step into it yourself
So why are you mad?
Why are you sad,
When you can be glad?
Why not? Whatever happens, happens
Nature will open her arms to hug you
To make you notice and appreciate her beauty
That she has brought upon the planet
Be inspired
Do things that inspire more people to do greater things
You have to be strong, be confident, be powerful
Because you are you
And that is the best thing you can be
To be happy, you have got to be kind to yourself and others
Make their day
That is the ultimate joy
So why not go outside? What are you waiting for?
Let's go today!

**Oscar Sasso (13)**
Hawley Hurst School, Blackwater

# TRAPPED

My task was almost complete
I was so excited about this new planet I had found
I was looking forward to returning to my home planet
With all the data I had collected

But here I am... trapped!
It seems that this strange human is gathering data from me
I'm confused by the language they use
And now I'm alone and locked in
I'm sad and long to return to my familiar lands

I've already tried to escape out of my cage
But it was no use
I'm terrified, all I want to do is escape
Or I wish I could trade places with one of the humans

I've started thinking how my family feel
I hope they don't come to see how I'm doing
I don't want them going through what I have.

**Olivia Marven (13)**
Hawley Hurst School, Blackwater

# MY TEARS

The harsh light,
The stiff bed,
The uncomfortable wires,
The never-ending trickle of a small saltwater tear
Dripping down the side of my face,
I hate this

My tired eyes,
My weak, fragile bones,
My racing heart all rolled into one,
I might think it is a few tears I am holding back,
But it's a tsunami of emotions,
Just trying to tear me down
And trying to ruin my hopeful mind,
I hate this

Why me, why anyone?
Why do my friends never visit anymore?
Why am I just sitting here while my friends are learning how to ride a bike,
While I am just learning how to stand on my own two delicate, fine feet?
I hate this
And I hope no one goes through this the way I did.

**Annabelle Fordham (13)**
Hawley Hurst School, Blackwater

# THE FUTURE POEM

A man who has nothing to do
But keep track of time
Travels in a box of night blue
And always flies
His companions are far from despair
Every time they travel
They always come back as a perfect pair
On several journeys
An intergalactic, unidentified object gets caught
In one of the ship's gurneys
When it's time to leave
This mysterious man starts to glow
When this man feels pain
It's time for him to go
With a new body, the man looks at his surroundings
He decides to fill his ship with his findings
But there's one question left unanswered
Who is this man and can you answer this question?
Doctor Who!

**Ruby Emma Welch (13)**
Hawley Hurst School, Blackwater

# WHAT IS THE DIFFERENCE?

Beginning of the year 2094,
One human was born,
That human was me,
My name is Emily

My best friend, Faith,
Has always been a mystery to me,
Never acting quite like us all,
Never looking any different

Never seeing her parents,
Faith always just seemed to vanish
Without even saying goodbye
My best friend, Faith

One day, the truth came out,
My whole life had been a lie,
The world turned upside-down,
My best friend Faith was a robot

Faith never ate, slept or drank,
All this time, she looked so real,
Why, my best friend, Faith?
Can you spot a difference?

**Lucy Chambers (13)**
Hawley Hurst School, Blackwater

# WAR OF HEARTS

Tears come to my eyes,
These once-brown eyes now blue
All these hidden lies,
No one knows what I've been through

Inside, I feel so broken,
Inside, my heart's in pieces
My words remain unspoken,
My love for him increases

Seeing them, I feel my heart shatter,
My world comes crashing down
I feel like I don't matter,
I smile just to hide my frown

They're happy together, what can I do?
I feel our friendship as it departs,
I can't say anything
Apart from 'I love you',
There are no winners in this war of hearts.

**Sofia Duggan (12)**
Hawley Hurst School, Blackwater

# THE CAT

I wake up, stretch, miaow and leap,
Some food and love are what I seek

My belly full, I'm ready for fun,
I creep outside into the sun

I sniff the air and look around,
Listening for every little sound

Something flickers, I'm ready to pounce,
Every little movement counts

My fur goes flat, I wiggle my back,
My breathing slows, ready to attack

My claws come out as fast as light,
I really want to win this fight

But it sees me and quickly flies away,
The butterfly wins another day.

**Sophia Wallis (12)**
Hawley Hurst School, Blackwater

# FREEDOM

I was once free,
But one day, it was taken from me.
Away it was taken
For the judge was mistaken.

Falsely accused was I
By a jealousy as quick as a fly.
A jealousy disgusting as gruel
Brought by a friend so cruel.

Stolen away was I
To rot in misery and die.
Why it did not work, you wonder why
Well, I tell you I still can fly.

Fly, you may ask?
Yes, it's a crazy task
But I fly
In my mind's eye.

I fly past stars so bright
Because I have freedom
As great as flight.

## George Benedict Herbert (13)
Hawley Hurst School, Blackwater

# WHY?

Why is everyone out for money?
Why does everyone want power?
Why are you doing this?
That's the question I'm asking

Why is everything about negativity?
Why is everything about who owes you what?
Why are you doing this?
That's the question I'm asking

Why do you build borders?
Why do you deny immigrants?
Why are you doing this?
That's the question I'm asking

Why is everyone always bragging?
Why have you got to have the new stuff?
Please just think of others and be grateful.

**George Allington (11)**
Hawley Hurst School, Blackwater

# THE ENDLESS BLACK ABYSS

The black nothing of space diverts Charlie,
A vast endless vacuum lies before
A time capsule that is forever,
Our planet like a pea in the void of space

Unkempt, unearthly spheres floating in an abyss,
Charlie marvels at its bliss
Shooting star roam the galaxy free,
Asteroids headed to distant solar systems

Black holes absorbing dark matter around them,
Stars in the background illuminate the infinite blackout
A small cluster of red stars dying, their light fading away,
Space is filled with devastating things.

**Oliver Hounsham (13)**
Hawley Hurst School, Blackwater

# MY DOG, STAN

I have a dog,
His name is Stan
He can run very fast,
Faster than I can
We go for long walks
And run through the trees
Stan jumps in the river,
We kick up the leaves
Far, far ahead,
A tree has fallen to the ground
We climb over the branches,
There are leaves all around
They are crispy and crunchy,
Coloured orange and yellow and red
Then the clouds grow darker,
I feel rain fall on my head
"Come on, Stan,
It's time to go back!"
We run home together,
Along the muddy track.

**Will Bennett (13)**
Hawley Hurst School, Blackwater

# SUMMER

Summer is here
Wasps are everyone's fear,
Singing, dancing, hear it all
Walking in the park, trees so tall
Ice-cold lollipops
Animals, insects and bunny hops
Busy places, swimming pools
Friends having lunch outside on stools
Everybody's having fun
Playing around in the sun
Girls dancing in the sun
With their hair up in a bun
We're near the end of summer break
Adults, children spend their last days at the lake
Ready for a new year to start
Students, teachers and their pumping hearts.

**Megan Glover (12)**
Hawley Hurst School, Blackwater

# ESCAPE

Terrifying cages in a lab
People everywhere
Grabbing you
Feeding you random things
Despair
Breaking your cage
Leaping across people
Breaking the window
And gone...
With a big breath of air
Primate escaping
Running extremely fast
Climbing, leaping
Hoping to clamber out
Without a care

Never happening...
The rush of pain
Flowing through your veins
Testing my soul
Ripping me to shreds...
You won't get out of here.

**Harriet Clowes (13)**
Hawley Hurst School, Blackwater

# ATLANTIS

Birds are singing in the breeze
The sound of the sea crashes next to me
I miss the land as it drifts away from me
*When will it come back?* I think as I sleep
The storm comes closer, is that a hand I see?
With coconuts and trees, I scream and shout
As the tree gets struck before me
I'm cold and wet as I fall into the sea
I sink and fall and I cannot breathe
I close my eyes and then I see a city under the ocean
In the deep sea.

**Louis Davies (11)**
Hawley Hurst School, Blackwater

# THE DARK

Dark is all I see
Blackness, it may be the last
A looming ash tree
From a dead hand of the past

Black dog on my shoulders
And each day it grows
Heavier than boulders
Icy wind, it blows

I know it's my time
My dreams keep me awake
I hear the bells chime
The tolling of heartache

There's a spark of light
It is worth holding onto
At least overnight
Light grows when thinking of you.

**Cameron Frain (12)**
Hawley Hurst School, Blackwater

# MY CAT, MILO

I have a cat called Milo,
He is very cute, don't you know?

He sleeps with me as the night goes by,
And I hug him tight as we lie

He hunts and kills and eats the mice,
Which is very messy and not very nice

He's ever so playful, some may say mischievous,
He nibbles my dressing gown and blue blanket

He is fluffy and squishy and cuddly to touch,
He is my best friend and I love him so much.

**Hennie Lamers (13)**
Hawley Hurst School, Blackwater

# A FRIEND LIKE YOU

You tell me something true,
I don't want to hear
Something crazy,
Like you've just had a beer!

You didn't throw me in the dumps,
When my problems were too tough
You put time aside for me,
When your life was rough

You are my best friend,
One of a kind
With your laughter and strength,
Together, we find
Life is fun all of the time!

**Alyssa Day (11)**
Hawley Hurst School, Blackwater

# WE NEED SOME CHANGES

The wars and the fights need to stop
The piercing fire of the gun
Hacks through each and every one
The shouting and the booing
Commences us all and we are done
We need to stop and think
Not just blink
The crimes and the lies
Have got to go
Just take a stroll around the block
The wars and the fights need to stop
The wars and the fights need to stop.

**Miah Greenslade-Jones (12)**
Hawley Hurst School, Blackwater

# WINTER

It is falling softly onto the grass,
All of the winter inhabitants coming out
The hares, deer and robins all out and about,
Lakes and ponds frozen solid
Ducks struggling across,
The snow is soft like cotton and white like glitter
People having fun throwing snowballs and building figures,
This is the best time of year
Wintertime is here.

## Zaynah Faruque (13)
Hawley Hurst School, Blackwater

# SERENA

There once was a girl named Serena
And she was once a brilliant winner
Making an issue out of her colour
Having recently become a mother
The umpire called her up for cheating
And she was very harshly disagreeing
Serena didn't find it fair
But showed Naomi no care
In the end, Naomi won
Serena still mad, but still gave her a hug.

**Lottie Hill (12)**
Hawley Hurst School, Blackwater

# SEXISM

Women are treated differently compared to men
They are always on the bottom
Everyone should be treated equally
No one should have different rights
Why are there more men in government?
Who is the ruler of England?
The Queen
Who is the Prime Minister?
A woman
We are all human, so let's stick together.

## Savannah Everidge (11)

Hawley Hurst School, Blackwater

# CHRISTMAS IS COMING

*Haiku poetry*

Christmas is coming,
Hurrah! Let's celebrate now,
Like opening gifts

Crackers detonate,
Santa has come and left gifts,
The food tastes divine

Christmas is over,
Tomorrow is Boxing Day,
Good luck for next year.

## Surya Ray-Chaudhuri (11)

Hawley Hurst School, Blackwater

# ADVENTURE

I am going on an adventure!
There are lots of things that you can do
You can climb the trees,
Or even look at bees
Look through bushes,
Go through tunnels
Go down one path and then another,
Because you are going on an adventure!

## William Carter (12)
Hawley Hurst School, Blackwater

# THE FUTURE

How mysterious it is,
But how many people care?
What it might be like,
Or if it is even there?

Every ounce of effort,
For something such little is known about.
Will it be full of peace and tranquillity?
Or of war and misery?

The future.
How bright it may seem to some,
How dark it may seem to others.
The future is a bigger mystery than the past.

Some say that the future will be great,
They say that it will be remarkable.
Somewhere where everyone will be accepted,
Somewhere that is advanced.

But do they know?
Every little decision
Is changing the future.
Everything that is currently happening,
Is setting the future

Every error, every mistake.
Everything will lead to the future.

This is inevitable.
The future is inevitable.

**Tareef Ahmed (14)**
Mayfield School, Portsmouth

# DEPERSONALISATION

I pulled myself apart limb from limb to see if there was
anything of substance left behind in the vacancy
With the abrasiveness of a child savaging a toy, and the
absence of sentiment exhibited by such a being
I did not bleed, for there was an insufficiency of humanity, I
looked at myself as if examining a corpse
She was a doll pulled inside out, vulnerable but childish and
uninhabited, leering at me probingly
She possessed no authority to examine me in such a way

I detachedly observed exuberant schoolgirls plastered in
second-hand singularity, unexpectedly assured
I noted pallid boys saturated with the delicateness of
moonflowers, exhibiting the steeliness unjustly acquired
I slipped in and out of characters and dispositions like
garments that refused to fit, swamping and unflattering
I tore them away, the same sentiment as wiping nitid teal
eyeshadow as the curtain drops behind you
But if I was going home, the location, if not unattainable,
was unclear

I was a nomad voyaging and finding hospitality in varying
places, none of which seemed willing to stick
My character was intangible, manufactured with the
presumptions of others by the hand of a stranger
My mentality was divorced from my figure but neither
belonged to me, they were heavy, oppressive masks

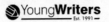

I would never come to unearth what lay underneath them,
until then I had to piece myself back together
Until then I would be floating, floating, floating.

### Emma Boddy (13)
Mayfield School, Portsmouth

# A SCENT-SUAL SONNET

I just need to tell you, I love your scent
Reminiscing gets me in my feelings
My constant love for you remains unbent
Partly 'cause you smell so damn appealing
My mouth waters at your glorious smell
More heavenly than the most precious pearl
My heart spins around like a carousel
Taste on my tongue making my senses swirl
My skin tingles, teased by your pheromones
And my body drowns, drenched in your aroma
I'm a miner and you're a precious stone
Me, an astronomer, you, a supernova
Grease, salt and brown paper, the sweetest perfume
Hot chicken and chips, alone in my room.

**Stefania Enciu (13)**
Orchardside School, Enfield

# FUTURE BOOK

This is a book which none shall find,
Words that will never cross your mind
Open me up and you shall see,
What is held in destiny

Go on, reader, take some breaths,
Because what beholds spells certain death
Take a peek and change your fate,
Take your time as it's always too late

Stay up reading throughout the night,
Addicted to your own morbid blights
But cheer up, reader, it's not all bad,
Some of my words will make you glad

The crystal balls are all in me,
So open my seal and set me free
There's really no need to tell me your name,
For in these chapters, you are famed

There's not a word you say that I don't know,
If you're hiding, my friend, you might as well show
I know your secrets, big or small,
There's nowhere to run, there's no one to call

So pick me up and take me home,
No one will know, we're all alone

Don't miss out, because in each verse,
I hold the secret of the world.

## Maliha Khatun (11)
Priory School Specialist Sports College, Southsea

# THE HAUNTED

*Haiku poetry*

Noises in the night,
Unexplainable movement,
That's a poltergeist

As the full moon rises,
Your inner animal wakes,
Howling for freedom

Craving blood since birth,
Hiding as bats during night,
They walk among us

Himalayan beast
Roaming the tallest mountains,
Mountain protector

Lurking in Loch Ness
Is the largest water snake,
Are the rumours true?

The forest hider,
Leaving trails of large footprints,
Cousin of legend

Luring boats to doom,
Hallucinating beauties,
Stay back from sirens.

### Blake Walker (15)
Priory School Specialist Sports College, Southsea

# THE DARK FUTURE

*Haiku poetry*

The world today is
A wonderful place, sort of
Don't forget one thing

The world is changing
We are making lots more things
And that won't help us

For instance, robots
They could rise up and hold us
Hostage till we die

Maybe rocks in space
Will crash into us at speed
I doubt we'd survive

But we still have hope
That won't happen for some years
Well, here is hoping.

## Ben Mansfield (12)
Priory School Specialist Sports College, Southsea

# AN ODE TO TIM BURTON

Mixing Halloween and Christmas,
The two best times of the year,
To create a twisted world of mystery

Creating a love story in-between the two,
The tale of Jack and Sally,
A true artist

Throwing the reader into a whole new world,
"One person's craziness is another reality,"
Said Tim Burton.

**Nellie Fraser (12)**
Priory School Specialist Sports College, Southsea

# THE FOX

The fox, the sly, sly fox
Slinking around in the night
Pilfering and pillaging was all he knew

And giving his neighbours a fright

On an inky black night
Many moons ago
He claimed a new territory
And moved into his dark, dark burrow.

**Xander Harris**
Purbrook Park School, Purbrook

# SEASIDE TRINKETS

I stride along the shoreline,
The sand passing through
My fingers,
As I reap the foamy waves
In search of seaside trinkets

A cracked, bloodstained jar,
The crevices full of scales,
A wrecked model of a boat
With torn and ruined
Sails

A beaten, battered jellyfish
Far from his family shoal,
Would he rather be dead upon
The beach,
Or hunted, swallowed whole?

There are many things the
Waves wash up
From far out at sea,
Trying to show us evidence
Of what our litter
Really means

I stride along the shoreline,
The sand passing through my fingers,

As I reap the shoreline
For seaside trinkets.

**Maisy Middleton**
Purbrook Park School, Purbrook

# SCOOTERS

There's a familiarity in the sound of scooters going over
bumps in the pavement,
I realised this as I sat on the curb next to my best friend,
Tucking our feet up as a small child whizzed past,
Our idle chatter stopped and all we could hear were the
bumps,
I guess in a way that's what a childhood sounds like

I remember the feeling as well,
The jolt that starts in your ankles and makes its way up,
Shaking your wrists as they grip the handlebars,
That same feeling every time

Nostalgia flooding your mind,
The continuous rumble it creates,
Going too fast and not slowing down,
Ominous paving slabs leering up,
As if they were made to throw us off

But even that now gives me a certain sense of happiness,
Then a graze on the knee,
Now a graze on the memory's surface,
A sound.
*Bump!*

## Robyn Louise Sage (13)
Queensbury Academy, Dunstable

# ODE TO SPRING

Spring mornings, life beginning to bloom,
A change from the cold, endless winter,
With the freshest smell of sweet perfume

Drifting up from the plants, the sweet perfume comes,
The beautiful pink blossom above drifting down,
While bees start to buzz and the hummingbird hums

Fluffy ducklings all in line following their mum,
Heading towards the sunlit, glittery pond,
Lounging in the early spring sun

New life entering the world for the first time,
Newborn lambs and fluffy ducklings,
Shuffle along through flowers in their prime

Spring is the best season, it seems,
Life starts to become full of colour again,
And the shining sun finally beams.

**Emma Pala (12)**
Queensbury Academy, Dunstable

# FITS AND STOPS

*Lipogram without the letter E*

*I* was told a lipogram was ludicrous without said 'you know what',
I watch my thoughts bypass this folio-
oh such futility amongst words!
This lipogram has withdrawn my right to lay on my pillow at night,
without rising hour upon hour-
black rings and I all too familiar companions.
I try so hard but my quill flows in fits and stops,
(unwilling to supply an obvious solution).
To think, I thought it was plain
How had I got it so wrong?
My fists in a ball,
my lips tight.
Why can I not acquaint ink with my thoughts?
My stomach churns with frustration as I try to think,
but my will to finish this lipogram will vanish,
along with all of this...

**Ella Molly Harris (13)**
Ratton School Academy Trust, Eastbourne

# WISH

*Haiku poetry*

Lively, humorous
You make me feel like I can
Fulfil all my dreams

Amiable, kind
You make me feel good about
The person I am

Bright, compassionate
You make me feel courageous
You give me purpose

Evanescent, gone
You don't realise I care
I'm invisible

Unworthy, wishful
I know I don't stand a chance
I should give up now.

**Billy Smith (14)**
Ratton School Academy Trust, Eastbourne

# THE FUTURE IS OURS

Our future is so unique,
It could never be bleak,
My future is tailored to me,
If you look, that's what you'll see,
There's a future out there for you,
It is everlastingly true

The future is like a maze,
Some choices put you in a daze,
Others have no effect,
And later on are wreaked,
Your destiny is your travels,
Your tale causes it to unravel

A future can shine as bright as a star,
As the present brings harm like a scar,
Pain can be found in a future,
Paired with wounds and suture,
But light can be found in darkness,
And we can be given mystical bliss

Our futures are a mystery,
A perfect combination of artistry
A path no one else walks,
A conversation no one else talks,
A scent no one else smells,

A tale no one else tells

The future is ours.

### Helen Marianne Knowles (11)
Swanmore College Of Technology, Swanmore

# MIDNIGHT

She runs through the forest
Tears in her eyes
Lost in her thoughts
Problems aside
Trembling with fear
Freezing at night
Nothing could help
She has to fight
Weak and abandoned
Broken inside
This is the end
I'm sorry
Goodbye.

## Aleksandra Kraszewska (14)
The Global Academy, Hayes

# SKY

I looked up at the sky and saw her,
Her beautiful eyes and silky hair,
How could someone be so cruel,
To a child as young as her?

An image of her came into my brain,
Seeing her face again gave me pain,
As I drew my eyes from the sky,
A clear liquid came to my eye.

I dared not to blink,
As I knew she wouldn't approve,
She hated sadness, along with madness,
And I had bravery to prove.

I went to my box of treasured things,
And took her last remaining thing,
Sky, my loving child, my everything,
It was time to say goodbye.

I took her gem outside,
And gave it one last kiss,
"Be free my precious Sky,
This is my last goodbye."

## Ashelyn Wangui Kahoho (12)
The Hazeley Academy, Hazeley

# I WISH THEY WOULD NOTICE ME

I wish they would notice me
the cooler people at school
I try to get their attention
but they think me a fool

I change my hair
they laugh
I change my clothes
they barf
so when I change my personality
they say, "You're the most stupid girl in class."

Inside I start to crumble
and boil and bubble
I hide behind the screen
and try my luck on social media

I make a fake account
and also change my name
hoping they will be nice
and like me again

Bottled up emotions whiz around my head
as I lie there, angry and shaking in my bed
I follow all their Instagrams, Snapchats and more

but they find out and carry on
no different than before

I appear back at school again
after taking a 'sick' day
the moment I enter my classroom
cold stares sting my face
I have made a massive mistake
I want to disappear out of this place

So stupid, so idiotic, I feel so bad
I run into the toilets and call my dad
I can hear their voices taunting and shouting
they keep on singing, "Come out you fatty."
If I don't come out, I'll be proving them right.

Then I wake up from my terrible dream,
what a night!

## Michelle Hanson (11)
The Hazeley Academy, Hazeley

# THE MONSTER UNDER THE BED

I am scared,
of the monster under my bed,
I know he's there,
ready to scare me,
his red eyes stare,
I know he's there.

I need a drink,
I am thirsty,
very thirsty,
but he's there,
I know he's there,
ready to scare.

I grab my teddy,
wrap my blanket around me,
I know he's there,
ready and waiting,
ready to scare.

I leap out of bed and run,
run through the bedroom,
dash across the landing,
I'm at the stairs and I screech to a halt,
and I stare,

I've forgotten about the other monster under the stairs.

I slide on my slippers,
creep down the stairs,
then I see the monsters,
I see them,
right there.

I dash into the kitchen,
turn on the tap,
grab a glass,
and fill it up fast,
then suddenly something
terrible happens.

I have to get back before 3am,
it's 2:59, if I make it back fast,
I could survive,
or the monsters will grab
then take me away,
I won't let that happen,
no, not today.

I grab my drink,
back up I go,
rapidly burning up the stairs, I know,
I get to the top,
I still went slow,
Oh no!

I've spilt all the water,
it took me so long to get,
so back down I go,

I grab some more water,
the monsters are there,
ready to slaughter,
then here I am,
with my cool glass of water,
I take a sip then fall asleep,
knowing that the monsters are unable to beat.

**Lily Connell (11)**
The Hazeley Academy, Hazeley

# WORLD WAR II

When life is unjust,
And there is no one to trust,
With the gun in your hand,
Still wondering why.

You are never too old,
To be in the war,
That is something we get told.

You go through the door,
And see the outer world,
People are dead,
That is a threat.

Months later, this would be over,
That's what we thought,
Well we were wrong,
More than three years this has lasted,
Until Hitler's now dead,
He shot himself in the head.

England has won,
Bletchley had helped,
We must celebrate,
That we are now safe.

**Laia Gomez-Ortega (11)**
The Hazeley Academy, Hazeley

# SOMETIMES I WISH

Sometimes I wish I was smarter,
Sometimes I wish I was stronger,
Sometimes I wish I was better,
Than who I am right now.

Sometimes I wish I was flexible,
Sometimes I wish I was someone else,
Someone who is more capable,
Someone in my wildest dreams.

Sometimes I wish I was amazing,
Sometimes I wish I was the best,
Sometimes I wish I was good at running,
But I'll put that dream to rest.

Sometimes I wish I could be myself,
Without any judgement,
What's the matter with that?

**Zahra Khota (12)**
The Hazeley Academy, Hazeley

# FIRE, FIRE

Fire, fire burning bright,
The red-hot sun pours with light,
The smoke fills the air tonight.

Poor animals, scared with fear,
I don't know what to do, let's wait and hear.

Fire, fire burning bright,
The red-hot sun pours with light,
The smoke fills the air tonight.

Fire, fire coming near,
Come on quick, get out of here!

In a shelter safe and warm,
No more fire, no more, no more.

Fire, fire burning bright,
No more fire of the night!

## Keira Goody (11)
The Hazeley Academy, Hazeley

# ADVENTURE NIGHT

Something happened one night,
I woke up in a fright,
Could it have been the light?
In my thoughts it was scary,
But the next night, I was going to find it,
I stayed up a little bit,
The night came,
My mum thought it was lame,
*Tick!* The clock struck,
Time was near but it lied,
It was monster time,
I heard it coming, *could it be lightning?*
It turned out it was just my brother snoring!
I thought it was a monster,
Life is unfair!

## Grace Thomas (11)
The Hazeley Academy, Hazeley

# THE EYES IN MY HANDS

The eyes in my hands,
Guide me everywhere,
The eyes in my hands,
Show me the way, though I don't know what's there,
They coax me into excitement, suspension at every turn,
Touching something unknown makes my stomach churn,
And then I trip, smack into a wall,
It's such a surprise for all,
My senses,
My real eyes open, my other ones close,
So I wander up the stairs,
And go into my room, hop into my bed and have a doze!

**Adam Scott (11)**
The Hazeley Academy, Hazeley

# MINE

Imagine if he gave me a rose
Oh, how I feel so alone
If only he gave me time
Then he would be mine
But I feel like he's telling me fibs

Saying he doesn't love someone within
Well this young fellow's hair is a bit yellow
Like the sun in the sky lifting me so high
But if only he gave me time
Then I could call him mine.

**Zenovia Kalyana (11)**
The Hazeley Academy, Hazeley

# THE DARKNESS OF THE RAINFOREST

In my sight are trees,
branches towering,
snakes hissing in every direction,
in the darkness are blood-red glowing eyes,
my heart's beating faster than a cheetah,
my breathing intensifies as I run.
Is this the end?
Am I dead?
"Time is up."
The man takes off the goggles,
it was only virtual reality...

**Yaser Hameed Kadhm (11)**
The Hazeley Academy, Hazeley

# THE WONDERFUL WORLD OF DISNEY

Disney is a world away,
let's go, hip hip hooray!
To infinity and beyond,
go and see the princesses waving their wands.

Go on the coasters for a thrill,
but some spinny rides will make you ill.
Get a Mickey autograph,
he will really make you laugh!

Candyfloss will make you happy,
but have too much and you'll wet your nappy!
There's Rapunzel and Cinderella,
I like the hair but not the cellar.

I wish the dwarves were my friends,
but now my day is at its end.

**Emma Sands (11)**
The Hazeley Academy, Hazeley

# THE MOON AND SEA

Whilst the moon decks herself in Neptune's glass,
And ponders her image in the sea,
Her cloudy locks smoothed on her face,
That she may be as bright as beauty be,
It is my wont to sit upon the shore,
And see with what grace she glides,
Her two concurrent paths of azure,
One in the heavens, one in the tides.

**Marta Lulka (12)**
The Hazeley Academy, Hazeley

# THE DEATH

I see a gaping hole,
a hole sucking in everything around it,
old, young, even babies,
a small hole I peek into,
torture and depression,
then a dark man,
grabbing men,
he is holding a scythe,
and then he drops to the floor,
so skinny, their heads thinned to skulls,
their arms so thin,
he is coming for me,
he does not honour my life,
no,
he grabs me, takes the wall,
the wall between me and death.

**Brandon Allun Delemere (11)**
The Hazeley Academy, Hazeley

# SADNESS

Sadness is a deep dark blue,
It spreads like pollution too.
Sadness can feel like a loss,
What makes it worse can be your boss.

Depression can hit you hard,
It feels like you've been hit by a car.
Dark clouds above your head,
You have feelings of dread.

Lots of things can make you sad,
Losses, let downs and others you've had.
Sadness is a deep dark blue,
Has anything sad ever happened to you?

**Gabriel Guimaraes (11)**
The Hazeley Academy, Hazeley

# HAKIUS

Winter

The snow is falling
Children are making snowmen
Snowballs flying through.

School

English, maths, science
Learning so much every day
English is the best.

Unicorns

Magical they are
Unicorns are amazing
Rainbows are their friends.

Stars

Shining in the sky
They are sparkly in the sky
A shooting star wish.

**Daisy Clark (11)**
The Hazeley Academy, Hazeley

# DISNEY PRINCESSES

Rapunzel, Belle and Cinderella
I love glass slippers but not the Cellar
Princess castles and fireworks, *bang bang!*
At the parade, oh the songs we sang

My fairy godmother waves her wand
I now have Rapunzel's hair, it's so blonde
Colourful bunting and fancy lights
Oh, it's ever so bright tonight

I with they were my friends
Disney princesses to the end.

**Stephanie Underhill (11)**
The Hazeley Academy, Hazeley

# BOOKS, TABLE GAMES, TEACHERS, FOOD

*Haiku poetry*

Books

Books are really fun
If they are a comedy
You will laugh a lot.

Table games

I like table games
I think they are really fun
Chess is the best one

Teachers

Teachers work at schools
They help you when you struggle
And make you smarter

Food

Food is good for you
Only if it is healthy
And has no sugar.

**Mikel Gomez-Ortega (11)**
The Hazeley Academy, Hazeley

# IF I COULD GO ON AN ADVENTURE

If I could go on an adventure
I would climb the highest mountain
Travel the vast ocean
Fly on a mythical Pegasus
Or go through an endless jungle
Or run through the hair-like grass
Adventures are really fun
Now start your adventure, one, two, three, go!
Or maybe you don't have to start your adventure
'Cause you're already on one.

## Mohammed Hassan Usman (12)
The Hazeley Academy, Hazeley

# I COULD WRITE A POEM

I have to write a poem
but I don't have a clue
I could write about football
or some monkeys in the zoo
I could write about my kittens
or how to tie my shoe
I could write about my brothers
or my best friends too
I could write about the sunshine
or how the sky is blue
And if you want me to
I could write about you.

**Ashton Phillips (11)**
The Hazeley Academy, Hazeley

# MORALS

Those who are fair deserve more,
And for karma to be in their favour,
But those who detest shall never stand out,
And stay just the way they are,
And those who love shall know,
The feeling will come and go,
And they shall never forget too,
So love those around you,
Your friends and family,
Go on and find love.

**Olivia Shane (11)**
The Hazeley Academy, Hazeley

# THE FUTURE

When I'm alone,
I always think,
What will the future be?
What will it be like?
Will there be hovering cars,
Or will we be flying to Mars?
Will there be pets,
Or robots as vets?
Will the world shrink,
Or will we even need to think?
I'm curious,
It could be hilarious,
The future!

**Keira Lee Galloway (11)**
The Hazeley Academy, Hazeley

# LIFE IS PRECIOUS

*Haiku poetry*

The past

He was always there,
Surrounded by protection,
But now he is gone...

The present

Enjoying my time,
Dancing and singing is life,
Flying all around!

The future

Strong and bold - stay safe!
Wrapped together in my arms,
Strengthening our love.

**Elissa Birkett (11)**
The Hazeley Academy, Hazeley

# THE FUTURE

The future world waiting,
Will it come or will it end?
Will it fight or will it bring peace?
Will it share or will it steal?
Will it multiply or will it divide?
Will it love or will it hate?
Will it starve or will it bring greed?
The future world, there we will be,
The future world waiting for me.

**Rhys Ingerfield (11)**
The Hazeley Academy, Hazeley

# DREAMING OF FISH

*Haiku poetry*

Wildest dreams come true
Lots of fish flooding the streets
Catch some, let one go

Look up in the sky
Fish like rainbows fly so high
Have three of its kind

Vendor passes by
Selling fish and fruit
Get them, share in parts.

**Charlie Preston (11)**
The Hazeley Academy, Hazeley

# Young Writers
## Information

We hope you have enjoyed reading this book – and that you will continue to in the coming years.

If you're a young writer who enjoys reading and creative writing, or the parent of an enthusiastic poet or story writer, do visit our website **www.youngwriters.co.uk**. Here you will find free competitions, workshops and games, as well as recommended reads, a poetry glossary and our blog. There's lots to keep budding writers motivated to write!

If you would like to order further copies of this book, or any of our other titles, then please give us a call or visit **www.youngwriters.co.uk**.

Young Writers
Remus House
Coltsfoot Drive
Peterborough
PE2 9BF
(01733) 890066
**info@youngwriters.co.uk**


Join in the conversation!
Tips, news, giveaways and much more!

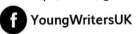 **YoungWritersUK**      **@YoungWritersCW**